ALL ROUND ENGLISH
1

Ronald Ridout
and Michael Holt

Illustrated by
Laurence Henry

Longman

STEP 1
What is it?

A This is a
Draw the picture.
Choose the right sentence for it.

1 This is a dish. ✗
  This is a fish. ✓
  This is a film. ✗

 ✓

1 This is a fish.

2 This is an apple. ✗
  This is the sun. ✗
  This is a football. ✓

 ✓

3 These are balloons. ✓
  These are apples. ✗
  These are footballs. ✗

 ✓

4 These are blots. ✗
  These are stars. ✓
  These are dots. ✗

✓

B What is it, then?

 1 This is not the sun.

 2 This is not the moon.

 3 These are not eggs.

 4 These are not footballs.

Draw the picture and write the sentence.
Then say what it really is.

1 This is not the sun.
  It is the moon.

C What's the word?
Copy the words and put a word for the picture.

1 This is the   1 This is the sun.

2 This is a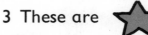

3 These are

4 These are

2

D Question time

Choose the right answer.

1 What is this?
It is a banana.
It is an icecream.
It is the moon.

1 It is an icecream.

2 What is this?
It is the moon.
It is the sun.
It is a star.

3 What are these?
They are apples.
They are bananas.
They are oranges.

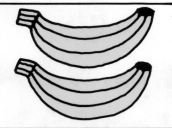

4 What are these?
They are apples.
They are stars.
They are bananas.

5 What is this?
It is a van.
It is a bull-dozer.
It is a bus.

6 What are these?
They are buses.
They are vans.
They are cars.

E What are they?

1 What are these things?
2 What is this?
3 What are these?
4 What is this thing?

5 What is wrong with the picture?

Can you find the answers here?
It is a tractor.
They are horses.
They are forks.
It is a cow.

1 They are forks.

F Can you answer them?

1 They are apples.

1 What are these?

2 What is this?

3 What are these?

4 What is this?

G Something to do

1 Draw a picture of a horse.
Under it say what it is.
2 Draw some cars.
Under them say what they are.

STEP 2

Birds, Insects, Fish

Birds

parrot   owl   robin

sparrow   duck

Insects

butterfly   fly   ant

wasp   ladybird

A What are they, then?

1 A robin is not an insect.
   It is a bird.

1 A robin is not an insect. ......
2 A fly is not a bird. ......
3 An owl is not an insect. ......
4 An ant is not a bird. ......
5 Sparrows are not insects. ......
6 Ladybirds are not birds. ......

B Bird or insect?

1 They are insects.

1 Are these birds or insects?

2 Are these birds or insects?

3 Is this a bird or an insect?

4 Is this a bird or an insect?

5 Are these birds or insects?

C Now try these?

1 It is an insect.

1 Is an ant a bird or an insect?
2 Is a duck a bird or an insect?
3 Are wasps birds or insects?
4 Are parrots birds or insects?
5 Is an owl a bird or an insect?
6 Are flies birds or insects?

D Say what these are.

1 A parrot is a bird.
2 Wasps are insects.

1 a parrot   3 owls   5 ladybirds
2 wasps   4 an ant   6 a sparrow

E What are they?

Copy the question.
Write the answer.

1 What are flies?
They are insects.

1 What are flies?
2 What are robins?
3 What is a butterfly?
4 What is a sparrow?
5 What are ladybirds?
6 What is a duck?

F Yes or No.

Choose the answers from these:
Yes, it is.   No, it isn't.
Yes, they are.   No, they aren't.

1 No, they aren't.

1 Are parrots insects?
2 Are ants insects?
3 Is a robin a bird?
4 Is a fly a bird?
5 Is an owl an insect?
6 Are ladybirds birds?

G Sort them out.

You can see four fish and four animals in this picture.
Draw a picture of them like the one at the top of the opposite page. Put all the fish in one part of your picture and put all the animals in the other part.

a cat
a sardine
an eel
a rat
a flying fish
a pig
a sole
a dog

H Can you answer these?

1 Is a sole a fish or an animal?
2 Is a rat a fish or an animal?
3 What is a sardine?
4 What are pigs?
5 Is an eel a fish?
6 Are flying fish birds?

I Something to find out

Write six sentences saying what each is—
a fish, a bird, or an insect.

1 eagle   3 mackerel   5 bug
2 shark   4 goose   6 beetle

5

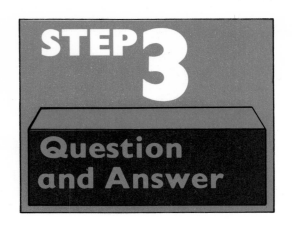

STEP 3

Question and Answer

I am Kate,
This is Ted.
I am seven,
He is eight.
We are saying hello,
Saying hello,
Saying hello to you.
We are saying hello,
Saying hello,
Saying hello to you.

Capital letters **ABCDE**

Small letters **a b c d e**

A full stop **.** A question mark **?**

All sentences begin with a capital letter.
A question sentence begins with a capital letter, and it ends with a question mark:
How old is Ted?

The answer sentence begins with a capital letter, and it ends with a full stop:
He is eight years old.

A Matching

Copy each question and match the right answer with it.

1 What is the boy's name?
His name is Ted.

The questions
1 What is the boy's name?
2 Is the girl's name Kate?
3 How old is Ted?
4 How old is his sister?
5 Who is Ted's sister?

The answers
Yes, it is.
He is eight years old.
His name is Ted.
Kate is.   She is seven years old.

B Asking questions

Ask Ted and Kate these questions, and let them answer. If you write them, be sure to put in the capital letters, the question marks and the full stops.

1 YOU What is your name?
KATE My name is Kate.

1 Ask the girl what her name is.
2 Ask the boy what his name is.
3 Ask Kate how old she is.
4 Ask Ted how old he is.
5 Ask Kate who her brother is.
6 Ask Ted what he and Kate are singing in the picture.

6

C Sentences

Write a sentence for each number in the picture of the dog.

These are the words you need:

nose   back   eyes   front paws
tail   jaws   ears   back paws

1 This is the dog's nose.
2 These are his eyes.

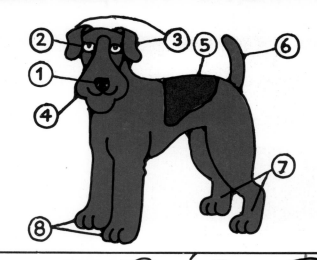

D What are they?

Ask a small boy called Tommy.

1 YOU What are these, Tommy?
   TOMMY They are faces.

E What is wrong?

There are ten things wrong in this picture. Write a sentence about each thing that is wrong.

1 The bicycle has only got one wheel.
2 ......

STEP 4
Yes or No

KATE My name is Kate.
      What is yours?
SCATTY My name is Kate.
KATE No, no, Scatty!
      That's my name.
      What is *your* name?
SCATTY Oh! My name is Scatty.
KATE That's right.
      Well done, Scatty! (He bows)
SCATTY (singing)
      Hello! Hello!
      I'm Scatty, I'm Scatty.
      I'm not Ted, I'm not Dick.
      I'm not Fred, I'm not Nick.
      I'm Scatty. That's me!
      Good-bye! Good-bye!

A Add a sentence

He is a puppet.
He got it right second go.
It is Kate.
It is Scatty
She is talking to Scatty
She is asking him what his name is.

Add to each of these sentences another from
the list at the top,

1 **The puppet's name is not Dick.**
  It is Scatty.

1 The puppet's name is not Dick. ......
2 The girl's name is not Jane. ......
3 Kate is not talking to Ted. ......
4 Scatty is not a real boy. ......
5 Kate is not asking him how old
  he is. ......
6 Scatty did not get the answer right
  first go. ......

B Question and answer
*Copy each question and match the right
answer with it.*

1 **Is the girl's name Scatty?**
  No, it isn't.

The questions
1 Is the girl's name Scatty?
2 Is the puppet's name Scatty?
3 Who is talking to the puppet?
4 Does Kate ask the puppet what his
  name is?
5 Does Scatty give the right answer
  first go?
6 What does Scatty say at the end of
  the song?

The answers
He says good-bye. Yes, she does. Yes, it is.
No, he doesn't.   No, it isn't.   Kate is.

8

TED
Can I fly, Ann?

ANN
No, you can't.

TED
Do I walk on four legs, Dick?

DICK
Yes, you do.

TED
Do I eat meat, Joe?

JOE
No, you don't.

TED
Are my ears very long, Bob?

BOB
Yes, they are.

TED
Kate, do I bray— Ee-aw?

KATE
Yes, you do.

TED
Am I a donkey?

EVERYONE
Yes, you are!

C Your replies

Pretend that Ted is still a donkey. Give your answers to his questions below.

1 TED **Am I an animal?**
2 YOU **Yes, you are.**

1 Am I an animal?
2 Can I climb trees?
3 Am I grey?
4 Am I very small?
5 Can you carry one in your arms?
6 Can I stand on my head?

D What about you?

Your answers must be true for *you*.

1 **No, I don't.**

1 Do you eat hay?
2 Do you like icecream?
3 Can you climb trees?
4 Are your eyes green?
5 Can you stand on your head?
6 Do you live in London?
7 Do you kick?
8 Are you a donkey?

E A game to play

Ask your teacher if your group can play the guessing game. The name is pinned on the back of the guesser so that he or she cannot see it. The guesser must ask questions that you can answer with yes or *no* till he can guess what it is.

| MONKEY | ELEPHANT | ANT |

STEP 5
Doing Things

A Draw and write

Choose the right sentence. Then copy the picture and write the sentence under it.

Kate is eating.
Ted is drinking.
Kate is drinking.

1

1 Ted is drinking.

Kate is swimming.
Ted is swimming.
Kate is diving.

2

Nick is painting.
Sarah is drawing.
Nick is writing.

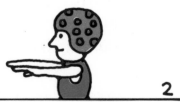

3

Nick is skipping.
Scatty is skipping.
Nick is running.

4

B What are they doing, then?
Add the right sentence.

**1 Ted is not eating.
He is drinking.**

1 Ted is not eating. ......
2 Kate is not swimming. ......
3 Nick is not writing. ......
4 Scatty is not running. ......

C Warm-up
How quickly can you answer these questions?

1 He is drinking.

1 Is Ted eating or drinking?
2 Is Kate diving or swimming?
3 Is Nick drawing or painting?
4 Is Scatty skipping or running?

D Who said it?
When the four children looked at the pictures, this is what they said:

1 Look, I am skipping.
2 That's me diving.
3 That's me painting a boat.
4 Look, I'm drinking coke!

Which child said which?

1 Scatty said this.

Peter   Ann   Simon   Linda   John

E What are they doing?

Here are the pictures of some more children.
Say what each child is doing. Choose the
right middle and end.

1 Peter is playing football.
2.......

Beginning	Middle	End
1 Peter	is pushing	an icecream.
2 Ann	is drawing	a cage.
3 Simon	is making	his bicycle.
4 Linda	is playing	a bus.
5 John	is eating	football.

F Who is doing it?

1 Ann is.

1 Who is eating an icecream?
2 Who is pushing his bicycle?
3 Who is playing football?
4 Who is drawing a bus?
5 Who is making a cage?

G What are you doing?

Ask the five children what they are doing
in the pictures.

1 YOU   What are you doing in the picture,
        Peter?
PETER   I am playing football.

H Make them true for you

Tom Best wrote these sentences.
Write some like them, but make them true
for you.

I am sitting at a small table, and I am
writing some sentences.
I am writing them with my new pencil.
Sally is sitting next to me.
She is reading a story book.
The teacher is talking to Bob in front.

I Free composition

Write about
what Scatty
is doing
in this
picture.

STEP 6
I Spy

A Yes or no answers

Ted is looking over the wall and Kevin is asking him questions.
Ted answers with Yes, I can. or No, I can't.

What does he say?

1 KEVIN Can you see any cows, Ted?
  TED   No, I can't.

1 KEVIN Can you see any cows, Ted?
2 KEVIN Can you see any aeroplanes?
3 KEVIN Ted, can you see any runways?
4 KEVIN Can you see any horses?
5 KEVIN Ted, can you see any trucks?
6 KEVIN Can you see any coaches, Ted?

B How many?

Now Kevin wants to know how many of each of these things Ted can see.
What does Kevin ask, and what does Ted reply?

1 helicopters	3 runways	5 aeroplanes
2 trucks	4 coaches	6 cows

1 KEVIN How many helicopters can you see, Ted?
  TED   I can see two.

1 one	·	4 four	::
2 two	··	5 five	:·.
3 three	·.	6 six	:::

12

C Say what you can see and how many

toys

kittens

birds

radios

frogs

1 I can see some bulldozers.
I can see two of them.

D How many did Ted see?

Say what Ted saw on his walk to the top of the hill—how many trees, horses, scooters, aeroplanes, gates, etc.

1 Ted saw two cars.
2 He saw four horses.

E Sentences

1 I can swim, but I can't dive.
I can ride a bicycle, but I can't ride a horse.

Ann wrote these two sentences. *Now you write five sentences like them about what you can do and can't do.*

F Something to write about
Write about the accident that Ted saw when he came to the trees with birds in it . . . .

G A game to play
Ask your teacher if you can play 'I Spy' like this:

IT I spy with my little eye something that is long, thin and yellow. I can see three of them. What is it?

PLAYERS Is it a ......? Is it a ......?
Is it a piece of chalk?

IT Yes, it is. Now you are IT, Ann.

STEP 7

Late for School

1

TED'S MOTHER Wake up, wake up!
Wake up, Ted!

1 Who can you see
  in the first picture?
2 Is Ted still asleep?
3 What is Ted doing
  in the second picture?
4 What is he doing
  in the next?
5 What is his mother
  holding in the next?
6 Does Ted
  have any breakfast?
7 Why does Ted think
  he is a clot?

2

TED Eh?
MOTHER Wake up!
It's nearly nine o'clock.

B Words

How many of these things
can you see in the pictures?
Make a list of them.
There should be 15.

3

TED Oh dear, I'm late.
Where are my clothes, Mum?
MOTHER Here they are, on the chair.
Quick, Ted. Hurry!
TED All right, Mum, I am hurrying.

bed	sheet
net	cake
chair	plate
hair	floor
table	door
desk	rook
arm	book
shoes	car
clothes	room
tree	school
feet	gate

4

MOTHER Here's your breakfast, Ted.
TED I haven't time for breakfast,
Mum, I'm late.

5

MOTHER All right, as you are so late you
can go to school without any
breakfast today. Good-bye, Ted.
TED Good-bye, Mum.

6

TED That's funny.
There is no one here.
The school is shut.
Oh dear, I remember now.
It's a holiday today.
I *am* a clot.

C Telling the time

The minute hand (long one) is pointing to 12. The hour hand (short one) is pointing to 7. What is the time? It is seven o'clock.

Now it is later. The minute hand has moved once round the clock face and is back to 12. The hour hand has moved from 7 to 8. It is now eight o'clock.

Now it is later still. The minute hand has moved right round the clock once more and come back to 12. The hour hand has moved from 8 to 9. Draw the clock and write the time under it.

D What is the time?

This is the same clock at different times during the afternoon—from just after lunch to about tea time. Copy the drawings and write the time under each one.

Choose from this list:

Now it is four o'clock.
It is one o'clock.
Now it is five o'clock.
Now it is three o'clock.

E Draw the clock

Draw a clock for each of these times:
1 It is six o'clock.
2 It is three o'clock.
3 It is four o'clock.
4 It is seven o'clock.

F Earlier or later?

This clock 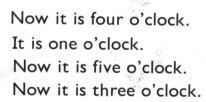 says it is one o'clock. Now it is an hour later.

The clock says it is two o'clock. Two o'clock is later than one o'clock. So one o'clock is earlier than two o'clock —it is an hour earlier.

Answer these questions.
1 Is two o'clock earlier or later than five o'clock?
2 Is four o'clock earlier or later than one o'clock?
3 Which is later, two o'clock or five o'clock?
4 Which is earlier, six o'clock or one o'clock.
5 How much later is five o'clock than three o'clock?

G A story to tell

Can you tell the story of how Ted was late for school? This is how Wayne started his story:

One day Ted's mother had to wake him up. It was very late. So Ted dressed as quickly as he could.

STEP 8
There Are

English

KATE Look at the word English on the board, Scatty. How many letters are there in it?

SCATTY There are six.

KATE No, no, Scatty! Count them.

SCATTY One, two, three, four, five, six, seven.

KATE How many letters are there in English, then, Scatty?

SCATTY There are seven.

KATE Well done, Scatty. *(He bows.)*

A Choose the right answer

1 **Are there five letters or six in <u>fight</u>?
There are five.**

Questions
1 Are there five letters or six in right?
2 How many letters are there in choose?
3 Is there a w in wrong?
4 Are there four letters in Dick?
5 Is there an a in kite?
6 Are there seven letters in Scatty?

Answers
Yes, there is.	Yes, there are.
No, there aren't.	There are six.
There are five.	No, there isn't.

B How many?
Ask someone how many letters there are in each of these words:

1 tug	3 late	5 night
2 pull	4 early	6 day

1 **YOU How many letters are there in <u>tug</u>, Ann?**
ANN There are three.

C Make sentences
Make six sentences by giving each beginning its right ending.

1 There are two es   in the word seat
2 There are five toes   in a week.
3 There are ten letters   on Andrew's foot.
4 There is only one e   in the word blackboard
5 There are seven days   in a year.
6 There are twelve months   in the word feet

1 **There are two es
in the word <u>feet</u>.**

D

Copy the sentence and say what the thing is.

1 It has two legs.
It is a bird.

1 It has two legs.
2 It has four wheels.
3 It has two hands.
4 It has four legs.
5 It has two wheels.
6 It has only one eye.
7 It has three legs.
8 It has four sides.

a stool

a needle

a bicycle

a square

a clock

a car

a horse

a bird

E A puzzle

Copy the puzzle. Then fit the right words in the squares. The first one has been done for you.

1	W	O	R	D	S	■
2						■
3				■	■	■
4						
5						■
6					■	■
7						■
8						■

1 There are many of these on this page.
2 There is often water in this.
3 This animal says mee-ow!
4 There are six letters in this word.
5 There are 64 in this book.
6 There are seven days in this.
7 There is a lot of sugar in this.
8 There are two os in the name of this seat.

cat
week
stool
sweet
words
finger
pages
glass

F Something to write

Write these words in two lists. Put all the five-letter words in one list. What have you in the other list?

write	puzzle	right	seven
letter	night	wrong	finger
early	wheel	horses	answer
needle	square	choose	eight

G Shadow play

Find out about your shadow. Then write a story or a poem about it. This is what Russell wrote:

My Shadow
What can you do, shadow? I can hop and jump and run and play. But only on a 'summer's' day. I can't sing like boys and girls can do. But I can nod my head and curl up too.

STEP 9
Colours

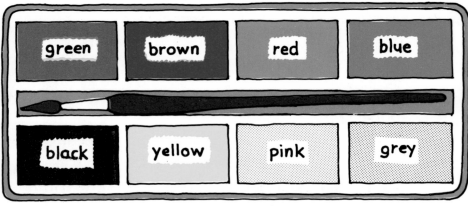

green brown red blue

black yellow pink grey

A What are they, then?
Add the right sentence.

1 The dog isn't brown. ......
2 The bus isn't blue. ......
3 The flower isn't red. ......
4 The cow isn't black. ......
5 The tractor isn't brown. ......
6 The car isn't blue. ......
7 The plane isn't pink. ......
8 The cat isn't white. ......

1 The dog isn't brown.
   It is grey.

B Which is?

1 Which is brown, the dog or the cow?
2 Which is red, the bus or the car?
3 Which animal is grey?
4 Which is pink, the flower or the bus?
5 Which of the things is blue?
6 Which is green?
7 Which is yellow?
8 Which animal is black and white?

1 The cow is.

C Asking questions

Ask someone
what colour
each thing is.

1 What colour is the cat, Jane?
   It is black and white.

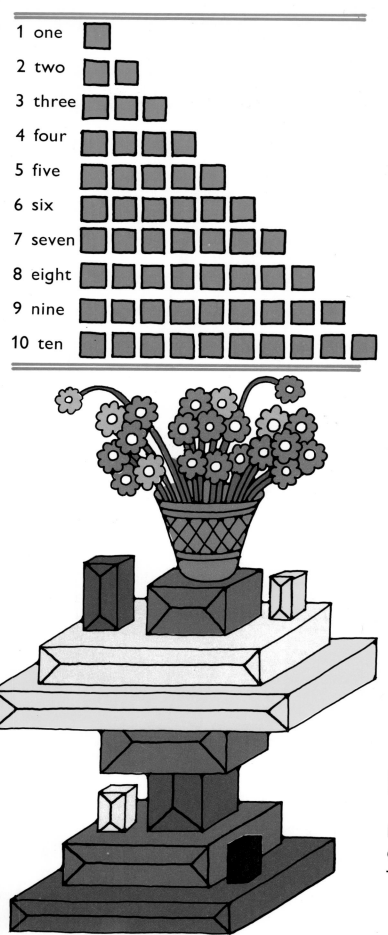

1	one	
2	two	
3	three	
4	four	
5	five	
6	six	
7	seven	
8	eight	
9	nine	
10	ten	

D Missing words

Put in the word for the missing number.

1 There are seven red flowers in the vase.

1 There are — red flowers in the vase.
2 In the pile there are — brown boxes.
3 There are — grey boxes in the pile.
4 In the vase there are — pink flowers.
5 There are — green boxes in the pile.
6 There is only — black box in the pile.
7 There are — tall blue flowers in the vase.
8 There is — small yellow box in the pile.

E How many?

1 I can see two.

1 How many yellow boxes can you see in the pile?
2 How many brown boxes can you see?
3 How many pink flowers can you see in the vase?
4 Say how many green boxes you can see.
5 How many red flowers can you see?
6 Say how many tall red flowers you can see.
7 Tell us how many grey boxes you can see.
8 How many tall blue flowers can you see?

F Something to do

Draw a pile of anything you like.
Colour the things in the pile.
Then write some sentences about them.

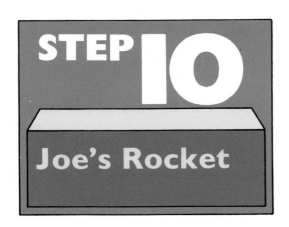

STEP 10

Joe's Rocket

Joe had a silver rocket. It was a good rocket, but it would not go. He tried hard to make it fly, but it still would not go.

Then one day Joe found a secret red button. He pressed it. The silver rocket shook and its door shut. It steamed and it hissed, and then it rose slowly into the air.

Joe put on his space suit. Then he said into the microphone: "Silver rocket, silver rocket, take me to the moon." The rocket suddenly swung round, and they were on their way to the moon. . . . Then they met a big jet plane. It was flying high in the sky. The jet tried to catch them up. But the rocket went too fast. Joe called back over his radio
"You can't catch me! You can't catch me!
I am flying higher and higher.
Ask me where I am going and I'll tell you.
I'm flying to the moon!—"

A Continue the story

What do you think Joe met next? Perhaps he met a space-ship, or a comet or a flying saucer. *Write what you think happened.* Then try to get the book called *Joe's Trip to the Moon* (Ridout and Holt, Purnell) to see what really happened.

B Sentences

You press buttons and ring bells. What do you do with the things below? *Give each beginning its right ending.*

1 You fly kites.

1 You fly	horses.
2 You kick	lights.
3 You eat	clothes.
4 You wear	footballs.
5 You ride	kites.
6 You switch on	sweets.

C Ask

Ask someone what you do with the things listed in B.

1 YOU What do you do with kites, Gary?
GARY You fly them.

D Question and answer

Choose the right answer to each question.

1 What colour was Joe's rocket?
It was silver.

Questions
1 What colour was Joe's rocket?
2 Would the rocket go at first?
3 What did Joe do to make it go?
4 Where did he want the rocket to go to?
5 What did they meet on the way?

Answers
He wanted it to take him to the moon.
He pressed a secret red button.
No, it wouldn't.
They met a big jet plane.
It was silver.

E What was the question?

Question
....?

Answer
It would not go.

What was the question?
It must have been: *What was wrong with Joe's rocket?*

Can you think what the questions for these answers must have been?
Choose the first three from the list. Make up the other two.

Questions
What did Joe tell the rocket to do?
Did the rocket go faster than the jet?
Did the rocket rise fast or slowly into the air?
......
......

Answers
1 It rose slowly into the air.
2 He told it to take him to the moon.
3 Yes, it did.
4 It tried to catch them up.
5 He was going to the moon.

21

STEP 11

How Many?

A Wheels

Look at the picture and then give each beginning its ending.

Beginnings	Endings
1 The scooter has	one wheel.
2 The van has	six wheels.
3 The wheelbarrow has	three wheels.
4 The car has	two wheels.
5 The truck has	four wheels.
6 The bicycle has	

B Ask how many

Ask a young boy called Joe how many wheels each has.

YOU   How many wheels has the
          wheelbarrow got, Joe?

JOE   It has one.

C More than, fewer than

The van has four wheels, but the scooter has two. So the scooter has fewer wheels than the van. The van has more wheels than the scooter.

Now complete these sentences:

1 The scooter has more wheels than ......
2 The car has more wheels than ......
3 The van has fewer wheels than ......
4 The car has fewer wheels than ......
5 The scooter has fewer wheels than ......
6 The ...... has the most wheels.
7 The ...... has the fewest wheels.

2 The car has more wheels than the bicycle and the wheelbarrow.

 Kate
 Ted
 Sarah
 Nick

D Questions

1 Nick has.

1 Which child has more cards than Kate?
2 Who has fewer cards than Sarah?
3 Has Ted or Kate more cards than Sarah?
4 Has Sarah or Nick fewer cards than Kate?
5 Which child has the most cards?
6 Which has the fewest?

E Scatty again

KATE   Arithmetic this morning, Scatty.
SCATTY Oh dear! Oh dear!
KATE   Nick has six cards and Sarah has four. How many more cards has Nick got than Sarah?
SCATTY Four more.
KATE   No, no, Scatty! How many more does Sarah need to make six?
SCATTY She needs two more. Oh, I see. Nick has two more than she has.
KATE   That's right, Scatty. *(He bows)*

Make up another conversation like this one with Scatty. Perhaps you could be Kate.

F Fewer or more?

Put in the missing number.

1 Nick has four more cards than Ted.

1 Nick has ...... more cards than Ted.
2 Ted has ...... fewer cards than Nick.
3 Nick has ...... more cards than Sarah.
4 Sarah has ...... fewer cards than Nick.
5 Ted has ...... fewer cards than Sarah.
6 Sarah has ...... more cards than Ted.

G Puzzles

There are two more cars than horses.

1 How many cars are there all together?
2 How many more cars than vans are there?
3 How many more horses than vans are there?
4 How many things in all are there—cars, horses, and vans?

STEP 12
ABC

| a b c d e f g h i j k l m |
| n o p q r s t u v w x y z |
| A B C D E F G H I J K L M |
| N O P Q R S T U V W X Y Z |

A Small letters

Write these words in small letters?

1 bottle

| 1 BOTTLE | 2 KETTLE | 3 LETTER |
| 4 FATTER | 5 ABSENT | 6 PRESENT |

B Capital letters

Now write these words in capital letters:

1 RABBIT

| 1 rabbit | 2 cabbage | 3 apple |
| 4 thinner | 5 babies | 6 ladies |

C Finish it

Continue each of these as far as you can.

1 P Q R S T ......
2 O Q S U ......
3 G H I J K ......
4 A C E G I ......
5 I H G F E ......
6 Z Y X W V ......

D Questions

1 G does.

1 Which letter comes just before H?
2 Which letter comes just after K?
3 Which letter comes just before T?
4 Which letter comes between D and F?
5 Which letter comes one from last?
6 Which two letters come between R and U?
7 Which letters come between D and G?
8 Which letters come after W?

E Alphabet sentences

Make an alphabet sentence for each letter of the alphabet. Choose your words from the list below.

1 A is for arrow.
2 B is for balloon.
3 C is for canoe .
4 D is......

eye	jug	paper	race
leg	donkey	uncle	face
shirt	zoo	toes	arrow
balloon	game	yellow	orange
mouth	icecream	hill	x-ray
wall	canoe	nest	vest
queen	kite		

F Making an ABC book

These sentences tell you how to make an ABC book. But they are in the wrong order. *Put them in the right order.*

fold once

You now have 32 pages.
Put them together and fold them three times.
Last of all, write the title on the cover.
Take two sheets of paper.
Staple the pages to keep them together.
Then slit the edges.

fold twice

fold three times

G Filling the ABC book

Write each letter of the alphabet on a separate page.
(How many pages do you need?)
Then draw a picture of the object that begins with that letter.
Under the picture, write what the letter stands for.

H h
H is for hammer

You will find all 26 objects in the pictures round this page. You can copy them if you like. Here are their names:

ladder	arm	car	kangaroo
hammer	van	foot	rocket
puppy	ball	queen	tractor
drum	mask	owl	zebra
umbrella	jug	nail	xylophone
wheel	egg	socks	igloo
gate	yacht		

Big, Bigger, Biggest

A Tall, taller, tallest

Scatty   Jack   The giant   The beanstalk

1 The beanstalk is.

1 Which of them is the tallest?
2 Which of them is the shortest?
3 Which of them is taller than the giant?
4 Which of them is shorter than Jack?
5 Which person is taller than Jack?
6 Which of them are taller than Scatty?

B Yes or no?

1 No, he isn't.

1 Is Jack as tall as the giant?
2 Is the giant as tall as the beanstalk?
3 Is Scatty the shortest?
4 Is the giant the tallest of all?
5 Is Scatty taller than Jack?
6 Are Jack and Scatty as tall as the giant?

C Missing words
Put in the missing words.

1 wide, wider, widest

1 wide	......	widest
2 slow	slower	......
3 short	......	shortest
4 high	higher	......
5 hard	......	hardest
6 dark	darker	......
7 big	......	biggest
8	thinner	thinnest
9 fat	......	......
10	......	hottest

D Finish them
Finish these as you think best.

1 A bus is bigger than ......
2 Elephants are the biggest ......
3 I am not as heavy as ......
4 Scatty is not as clever ......
5 A mouse is bigger ......

E Finish it

Look at the picture carefully, and then finish each beginning below. Use one of these words in each sentence: darker, smaller, bigger, taller, shorter.

I The farmer is bigger than the children.

1 The farmer is ......
2 The girl is ......
3 The boy is......
4 The minnow is ......
5 The farmer's hat is ......
6 The girl's hair is ......

F Ask

Ask someone what is (1) the biggest, (2) the smallest, (3) the tallest, (4) the wettest, (5) the hottest, (6) the hardest, (7) the softest, (8) the brightest thing he or she can see in the picture.

> **YOU** **What is the biggest thing you can see in the picture, Ann?**
>
> **ANN** **The biggest thing I can see is the lake.**

G Draw

Our artist has got his sizes wrong in the picture below. *See if you can draw the picture again so that the sizes are about right. Below your picture write how tall you think each thing is in real life. Tom Thumb was as tall as a man's thumb, actually!*

H Write

Look at the picture of the boy and girl fishing. Then write about what you think happened next.

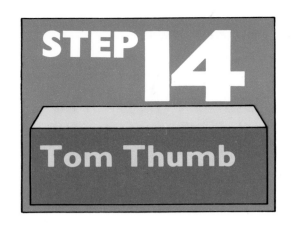

STEP 14

Tom Thumb

Tom Thumb was no bigger than a man's thumb, and he never grew any bigger. He was just 6 cm tall. His mother often left him to play on top of the kitchen table, because she could then keep an eye on him.

One day Tom's mother was making a pudding in a bowl. In the middle of mixing it, she was called away to answer the door. Tom was inquisitive like any other child. He saw the bowl and wanted to know what was in it. But of course he wasn't tall enough to see inside the bowl.

There was a fork lying on the table. Tom dragged this along and, after a struggle, got it up against the bowl. Then he swarmed up it, till he was able to look over the edge.

"What can it be?" Tom said to himself. "I must have a closer look." So he caught hold of the rim of the bowl and pulled himself up onto it.

He lay flat on the rim. Then he leant over as far as he could, so as to dip his fingers into the pudding mixture.

Suddenly Tom lost his balance and let out a tiny scream as he began to fall. Head first he went, right into the middle of the sticky pudding!

A Questions

1 How big was Tom Thumb?
2 Was he as tall as the mixing bowl?
3 Was he as tall as an egg?
4 Why did his mother leave the mixing bowl on the table?
5 Was Tom too short to see over the edge of the bowl?
6 Why did he set the fork up against the bowl?
7 Why did he climb on to the rim?
8 What was he doing when he fell in?

B Which are used in cooking?
Make a list of the six things that are used.

nails   flour   grass   milk   pens
bowls   sugar   water   stones   spoons

THUMB   SIDE
FLOOR   LIKE
DOOR   FLAG
LAMB   FLAP

C Can you do better than Scatty?

Answer these questions about the words on the board.

1 SIDE does.

1 Which word begins with S?
2 Which one begins with D?
3 Which one ends with T?
4 Which one ends with P?
5 Which ones begin with L?
6 Which ones end with E?
7 How many begin with F?
8 How many end with Z?

D Asking questions

Ask someone what each of these words begins with and ends with:

1 paint	3 cook	5 hide
2 faint	4 shook	6 slide

1 YOU What does the word *paint* begin with and end with, Joe?

   JOE It begins with P and ends with T.

E Something to write about

Write about what you think happened to Tom after falling into the pudding. (Did his mother hear him scream? How did she get him out? How did she clean the pudding off? How did Tom feel?)

KATE   What does thumb end with, Scatty?

SCATTY   It ends with m

KATE   No, no, Scatty.
Look at the board.
What does thumb end with?

SCATTY   Oh, I see. It ends with b.

KATE   Yes, the b is silent.

SCATTY   Like me!

KATE   How do you spell floor, Scatty?

SCATTY   f-l-o-r—floor.

KATE   No, no, Scatty. Look at it.

SCATTY   I am looking at the floor.

KATE   No, I mean the word.
How do you spell it?

SCATTY   f-l-double o-r—floor.

KATE   That's better. *(He bows)*

F Scatty lists

We asked Scatty to make three lists of these words. In the first list he had to put all the words that begin with S and end with E; in the second he had to put all those that begin with S and end with T; in the third those that begin with S and end with L. He didn't do it very well, did he? *Can you do it properly for him?*

side	slot	shell
spot	still	sport
save	sweet	spill
spell	shine	simple

STEP 15

Where?

C Where are they?

Ask someone where each child in the picture is.

1 YOU Where is James, Tom?
  TOM He is under the go-cart.

A Where are they, then?

1 She is behind it.

1 Kate is not in front of the crate. ......
2 James is not on the go-cart. ......
3 Charles is not behind the crate. ......
4 Emma is not under the go-cart. ......
5 Ted is not on the pipe. ......

B Who?

1 Ted is.

1 Who is in the pipe?
2 Who is under the go-cart?
3 Who is on the go-cart?
4 Who is behind the crate?
5 Who is in front of the crate?

D Writing sentences

Say where each child is.

1 Kate is behind the crate.

E Alphabetical order

Look at the first letter of each word, and then write the list of words in the same order as the alphabet.

1 boy, crate, girl, pipe, toy

1 pipe, girl, boy, crate, toy
2 James, Emma, Charles, Ted, Kate
3 chair, bed, sofa, table, desk
4 toy, girl, crate, pipe, toy

F Hide and Seek

Sarah is 'he' and the others are hiding in these places:

behind a bush
in the shed
up the tree
on the roof of the shed
under the steps

Write a sentence to say where each child is hiding.

1 Emma is hiding up the tree.

G Where are you hiding?

Pretend you can ask the children where they are hiding. Give their answers.

1 YOU Where are you hiding, Kate?
KATE I'm hiding in the shed.

H Where did you hide?

The game is over. You want to know where the children hid. *Ask them.*

1 YOU   Where did you hide, Charles?
CHARLES I hid behind a bush.

I A large bed

*Draw a bed, like this, but much bigger.
Draw Ted in the bed, Kate under it, the cat on Ted, Emma behind the bed, and James in front of it.*

Then write sentences to say where they all are.

J Your own picture

Draw your own picture with children in it. Say where they are and what they are doing.

STEP 16

Jobs

postman — Mr Jones
nurse — Mrs West
shepherd — Mr Brown

typist — Miss Green
miner — Mr North
pilot — Mr Adams

A What are they, then?

Add the right sentence.

1 Mr North is not a postman.
He is a miner.

1 Mr North is not a postman. ......
2 Miss Green is not a nurse. ......
3 Mr Jones is not a miner. ......
4 Mr Adams is not a shepherd. ......
5 Mrs West is not a typist. ......
6 Mr Brown is not a doctor. ......

Shepherds look after sheep.
Nurses look after people who are ill.
Typists write letters on typewriters.
Pilots fly aeroplanes.
Postmen deliver letters and parcels.
Miners dig for coal.

B What are you?

Ask each person what he or she is.

1   YOU What are you, Mr Jones?

MR JONES I am a postman.

C Who does what?

1 The shepherd does.

1 Who looks after sheep?
2 Who delivers letters?
3 Who flies aeroplanes?
4 Who looks after people when they are ill?
5 Who digs for coal?
6 Who types letters?

D What do you do?

Ask the people in the pictures what they do.

1   YOU What do you do, Mr Jones?
MR JONES I deliver letters and parcels.

E Alphabetical order

Arrange each list in alphabetical order:

1 teacher, doctor, actor, pilot
2 miner, farmer, carpenter, shepherd
3 grocer, baker, tailor, chemist

F Riddles

Can you say what each is?
This is how you spell their names:

jockey   footballer   shepherd
chemist   ironmonger   mechanic

1 He sells medicine. What is he?
2 He sells tools, nails, saucepans, knives and forks. What is he?
3 He rides race horses. What is he?
4 He earns his living by playing in matches. What is he?
5 He works on cars. Sometimes he repairs them. Sometimes he services them. What is he?
6 He looks after sheep. What is he?

G Make up a riddle

Make up five riddles of your own like those in F. They can be about anyone you like, such as a dancer, a miner, a bus driver, a clown, a pop singer, a film star, a fisherman . . .

H What's your line?

Find out what these people are by putting the letters in the right order.
The first is FARMER.

1 A. R. MERF   4 C. T. RODO
2 N. RIME   5 N. C. LOW
3 J. C. YOKE   6 I. P. LOT

I Science notes

A scientist looks at things around him. He also makes things happen and notes what he finds. Then he thinks about what he has found. *You try these things.*

1 Put a boat in a bowl of water. Better do this in the sink. What happens to the water? Does it go down? Does the boat make waves? Write down just what you see. Then put a stone on the boat. What happens? Maybe your friends don't see the same as you do. Don't worry. Write down what *you* think happens.
2 Next time you are near the swings, set an empty one swinging. Then get on a swing next to it and start swinging yourself. When you are as high as the other swing keep quite still. Which of the two swings goes up and down faster? Write down what you thought would happen, and then what actually happens.

J Someone to write about

Choose any person you like—a pop singer, a doctor, a pump attendant, a footballer, a teacher, anyone. Write some sentences to tell what the person does.

33

STEP 17

Days of the Week

1st	first	Sunday
2nd	second	Monday
3rd	third	Tuesday
4th	fourth	Wednesday
5th	fifth	Thursday
6th	sixth	Friday
7th	seventh	Saturday

A Warm up

1 Tuesday is.

1 Which is the third day of the week?
2 Which is the first day of the week?
3 Which is the sixth day?
4 Which is the fourth?
5 Which is the second?
6 Which is the last?

B Missing Words

Put the missing word in each sentence.

1 ...... is the fifth day of the week.
2 Monday is the ...... day of the week.
3 The sixth day of the week is ....
4 The ...... day of the week is Sunday.
5 Saturday is the ...... and last day.

C Before and after

1 Wednesday does.

1 Which day comes directly after Tuesday?
2 Which day comes directly after Sunday?
3 Which comes directly before Friday?
4 Which comes directly before Monday?
5 Which day comes directly after Sunday?

D Sentences to write

Write a sentence about each day.
Say which day it comes after and which day it comes before.

1 Sunday comes after Saturday and before Monday.

E How many?

1 There are five.

1 How many days are there after Monday?
2 How many days are there after Friday?
3 How many are there before Tuesday?
4 How many are there in a week?
5 How many are there between Monday and Friday.

F Finish it

What will the day be tomorrow?

1 It is Monday today, so it will be Tuesday tomorrow.

1 It is Monday today, so ......
2 It is Friday today, so ......
3 It is Tuesday today, so ......
4 It was Thursday yesterday, so ......
5 It was Sunday yesterday, so ......

G Finishing order

These six children had an egg and spoon race last Friday. *Say who finished first, second, third, fourth, fifth, last.*

1 Bob finished first.

H Ask

Ask the children where they came, in this order:

1 Karen	3 Bob	5 Ted
2 Will	4 Jane	6 Lesley

1 YOU   Where did you come, Karen?
KAREN I came fifth.

I Cheat!

Bob cheated. He wasn't counted after all. Who, then, was first? Who was second? And so on?

J Your race

Have you taken part in a race or watched one recently? Say what happened. (What sort of race was it? Where was it? When was it? How many took part? Did you overtake anyone? Did anyone overtake you? Did anyone fall over? Did anyone cheat? Who won? Where did you come?)

A game to play

Ask your teacher if four of you can do this. Each cut out seven small cards of the same size. On them write the day of the week—one on each card. Play Snap! with the cards. The game ends when one player has won all 28 cards.

Another game

Play 'Next day after' Snap with the cards. Jane plays Tuesday, Ron plays Wednesday Ron has the 'next day after' Tuesday. He calls Snap! and wins Jane's pile of cards.

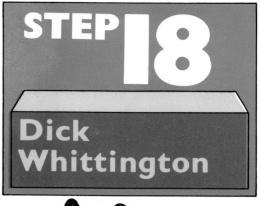

STEP 18

Dick Whittington

A long time ago there was a little boy, and his name was Dick Whittington. He lived in a village with his mother and father. But his mother and father both died, and Dick was left without money or friends. So he made up his mind to walk to London to seek his fortune there.

He put his few things in a little heap and tied them all up in a big red handkerchief. He fixed this bundle on the end of a stick, put the stick over his shoulder, and set out.

As he walked along, he thought about London. What a wonderful city it must be! He had heard that its streets were not made of stone like other streets. London streets were made of gold. Dick felt sure that he would grow rich in such a wonderful place as that.

But London was many, many miles away. Dick walked on and on. He felt very lonely. There was no one to talk to, and there was no one to help him. As he walked on, he begged for bread to eat, and he begged for water to drink. At night he slept in haystacks and barns. He was all alone and not very happy. Then something nice happened. He met a little cat.

Dick stroked the cat and made a fuss of her. She trotted along by his side, with her tail in the air. At last Dick thought it was time the little cat went home, or she would get lost. "Go home! Go home, pussy!" he said. But the cat did not go home. She just stayed there with Dick, rubbing against his legs and purring.

"All right," said Dick. "You can stay with me if you like. I am going a long way, and your paws may get tired. I cannot promise you fresh milk to drink, and I cannot promise you fish to eat, but you can share everything I have myself."

So the two walked along together, the cat keeping close to Dick's side.

A How well did you read it?

1 Where did Dick live?
2 How did he come to have no money?
3 Where did he decide to go?
4 What did he hope would happen in London?
5 How did he carry his belongings?
6 What wrong idea did Dick have about London?
7 How did he get food on the way?
8 Where did he sleep at night?
9 What was the nice thing that happened to him on the way?
10 How did it happen that the cat went along with Dick?

B What are they made of?

Streets are made of stones.

Make five sentences like this from the following:

1 Tables		rubber.
2 Bottles		wood.
3 Shirts	are usually made of	glass.
4 Books		cotton.
5 Tyres		paper.

C Something to find out
Find out what each of these things is made of.

| 1 shoes | 3 socks | 5 houses |
| 2 desks | 4 comics | 6 erasers |

1 Shoes are usually made of leather.

D Finding out

1 Gold would not be much good for paving streets because it is too soft and slippery. Which of these things would be hard enough to pave streets?

plasticine	mud
stones	plastic (hard)
bricks	plastic (soft)
paper	wood
iron	copper pennies

2 Try to find samples of the ten things. How can you tell which is the hardest?
3 Which of the things can you dent with a pencil?
4 Which of them can you scratch with a nail?
5 Write down the names of the ten things in order of hardness.

E A story to tell
Do you know the whole story of Dick Whittington? If you don't, you can read it in a lot of different books. Here is the name of one of them:
Look Ahead Readers, Book I (Heinemann).
When you know the story well, choose one of these parts to tell in your own words:

1 Tell about Dick's job as a kitchen boy.
2 Tell about how he ran away and was then called back by Bow Bells.
3 Tell about how Dick's cat made him a fortune by killing the rats and mice for the King of the Blackamoors.

STEP 19
Positions

A Warm up

1 James is.

1 Who is in front?
2 Who is right behind?
3 Who is between Bob and Emma?
4 Who is directly behind Sarah?
5 Who is directly in front of Bob?
6 Who is behind Bob?
7 Who is behind James and in front of Emma?
8 Who is in front of no one?

B Behind and in front of
Write a sentence about each child. Say who he or she is standing in front of and who behind.

1 James is standing in front of Sarah and behind no one.
2 Sarah is standing in front of Emma and behind James.

C Nearest, farthest
Sarah is farther from Bob than she is from Ted. Who is farthest from Emma? Try each child. You will find that Kate is farther from Emma than any of the others. So Kate is farthest from Emma.

Put in the missing names in these sentences.

1 ...... is farthest from James.
2 James is farther from Emma than from ....
3 ...... is the nearest to James.
4 ...... is farthest from Bob.
5 ...... is nearest to Kate.
6 Kate is nearer to ...... than to Ted.

D Look and think

1 Is Sarah farther from Bob than she is from James?
2 How many children are standing between Sarah and Bob?
3 How many girls are there behind James?
4 Is Sarah the nearest girl to Kate?
5 Which girl is farthest from Sarah?

E Put them in order

These sentences tell the story of the
pictures, but they are in the wrong order.
Write them in the proper order.

He called out for help.
She brought him safely to land.
Tommy's big sister took him to the park.
His sister dived in to the rescue.
He sailed his new boat on the lake.
He leaned over too far and fell
   into the water.

F

Write these sentences in their proper order.
There are no pictures to help this time.

Then they went from the swings to the
   bumper cars.
They walked home each proudly carrying
   a coconut.
One day Kate and Ted went to the fair.
After that they had a go at the
   coconut shy.
They had a ride on the swings first.

G

Here are some more sentences to write
out as a story. What do you think
happened next? *Write some more sentences
of your own.*

There were no eggs in it.
When Sarah visited the nest last Saturday,
   there were five baby birds in it.
There were five blue eggs in it this time.
About a month ago Sarah found a nest in
   the garden.
The mother bird sat on the eggs for about
   three weeks.
A few days later she visited the
   nest again.

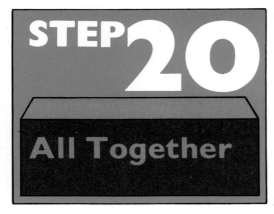

STEP 20

All Together

1	one	6	six
2	two	7	seven
3	three	8	eight
4	four	9	nine
5	five	10	ten

James   Emma   Bob   Kate   Ted

A Warm up

Count the balloons and answer the questions.

1 She has five green ones.

1 How many green balloons has Kate?
2 How many red ones has James?
3 How many blue ones has Emma got?
4 How many balloons has Ted all together?
5 How many has Bob got all together?

B Red balloons

Say how many red balloons each child has.

1 James has four red balloons.

C Who?

1 Emma has.

1 Who has the most blue balloons?
2 Who has the fewest green ones?
3 Who has no blue ones?
4 Who has the most green ones?
5 Who has the most balloons all together?
6 Who has the fewest all together?

D Blue balloons

Ask the children in the pictures how many blue balloons they have.

1 YOU   How many blue balloons have you, James?

JAMES I have one blue one.

40

E Put into figures

Here are some stories.
Write them as sums.

a 5+4 = 9

a Karen had five sweets. Wayne gave her four more. She then had nine all together.

b Stephen had 1p. He earned 2p more. He then had 3p all together.

c Carole had three cards. She found three. She then had six in all.

d Will had two marbles. He won two more off Tom. Then he had four all together.

e Ann ran 2 kilometres on Monday and 3 kilometres on Tuesday. She ran five kilometres in all.

F Put into words

Now make up stories about these sums.

1 Kate had three records. Ted gave her four more. She then had seven all together.

1 3+4 = 7
   (Ted gave Kate four more records.)
2 2+3 = 5
   (Ann found three more cards.)
3 3+1 = 4
   (John gave Linda one more toy car.)
4 4+2 = 6
   (Karen walked 4 kilometres on Wednesday.)
5 2+5 = 7
   (Dawn found 5p on the ground.)

G Tell the story

Say what happened at the circus. You will find the words in the list useful.
This is how Ted began:

The clown jumped through a paper hoop. The chimp copied the clown and jumped through a paper hoop, too . . .

waved	along	head
spectators	idea	laughed
fetched	poured	soaked
umbrella	water	tight-rope
opened	walked	

STEP 21

Making Things

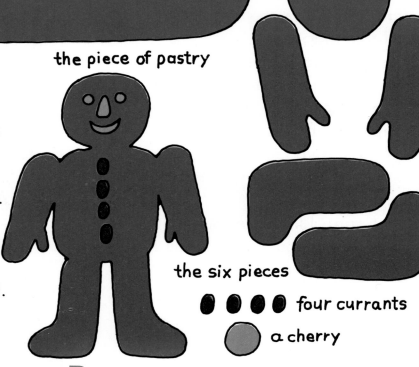

the piece of pastry

the six pieces

four currants

a cherry

It was very wet last Saturday,
and Kate had to play indoors.
Her mother was making an apple tart
for dinner. She gave Kate
a piece of the pastry.
"I will make a pastry man," said Kate.
So she cut the pastry into six pieces.
With the biggest piece
she made the pastry man's body.
With the next piece she made his head.
Then she rolled two small pieces
into the shape of arms.
There were then two pieces left.
She made those into legs.
Kate took four currants
and gave the pastry man four buttons.
For his eyes, nose and mouth she cut
up bits of red cherry. Then she put him in
the oven and baked him.

A Questions

1 Why did Kate have to play indoors?
2 Who gave her the pastry?
3 What did she make with it?
4 What did she use for the body?
5 How did she make the arms?
6 What did she make the mouth from?

B Putting sentences in their right order

Put these sentences in the same order as Kate did the things.

1. Then she made the head from the next piece.
2. Last of all, she made the eyes, nose and mouth from a cherry.
3. Kate cut the pastry into six pieces.
4. She made the last two pieces into the legs.
5. She made the body from the largest piece.
6. After that she made the arms from two small pieces.
7. Then she stuck on four currants for buttons.

42

C Scatty's diary

Find all Scatty's mistakes. Put them right, if you can.

Number words I know
two noe ixs eight inne

Date...60th June

This morning I had 6 marbles.
I played marbles with Kate.
She won two marbles off me.
So now I have 2 marbles more
than I began the day with.
Kate tells me that tomorrow
is 24th July. That means
Christmas is nearly here.
I bet she'll give me some
marbles then. Ate three cakes
and then two more. That made
six cakes in all. Felt sick. Went
to bed early at 3 o'clock in the
afternoon. Three hours later
I felt better and got up. It was
five o'clock. Had tea with Kate.

D Something to do

Take a sheet of paper.
Fold it once.
Fold it again.
You have now got
four corners.
Draw something lopsided
in one corner.
This is what
        Scatty drew
Fold the sheet and hold it
up to the window.
Trace the picture you can
see showing through.
Unfold and fold again
another way. Trace
what shows through.
When you have filled
all the corners, you
should get something
            like this
Lay a mirror along each of the folds.
Write down what you can see.

E Making a paper boat

*Explain how the boy in the poem made a
boat from a sheet of paper.*

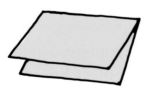

the folded sheet

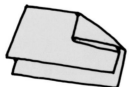

the first corner
folded back

both corners
folded back.

the boat afloat.

A sheet of paper

I could paint a picture
  Blue and green,
The sky and the sea
  And some rocks in between.

I could draw a witch
  And a witch's house.
And a witch's cat
  With a witch's mouse.

No. I'll fold it over.
  And make a boat.
And in my pool
  I'll set it afloat.

RUTH AINSWORTH

43

STEP 22
Birthdays

Alex · Kate

Tom · Sam

Linda · Jane

A Ages

Kate is seven today.
Five of her friends have their birthdays today, too. But they are not the same age as Kate. *Say how old each of the children is.*

1 Alex is twelve years old today.

B Warm up

1 She is eleven.

1 How old is the oldest child?
2 How old is the youngest boy?
3 How old is Linda?
4 How old is the oldest boy?
5 How old is the youngest girl?
6 How old is the youngest child?

C Ask

Ask the children how old they are today.

1 You How old are you today, Alex?
  ALEX I am twelve today.

D Which of them?

1 Jane is.

1 Which of the girls is older than Sam?
2 Which of the boys is younger than Kate?
3 Which of the children is the oldest?
4 Who is the youngest?
5 Which is the youngest girl?
6 Which is the oldest boy?
7 Which girls are younger than Sam?
8 Which of the boys are older than Linda?
9 Which of the girls are younger than Tom?
10 Which boy is younger than the youngest girl?

44

E Add the right sentence

1 August is not the ninth month.
It is the eighth.

1 August is not the ninth month. ......
2 October is not the eleventh month. ......
3 July is not the sixth month. ......
4 November is not the tenth month. ......
5 December is not the eleventh month. ...

F A list

Complete this list.

1 January is the first month.
2 February is the second month.
3 March is ......

G Birthdays

Name	Birthday
Ted	13th July
Vicky	2nd February
Dawn	10th December
Richard	3rd January
Joanna	7th October
Matthew	1st September

We write *7th October*, but we say *the seventh of October.*
Say when each child has his or her birthday.
Then write it.

Spoken
1 Ted has his birthday on the thirteenth of July.
Written
1 Ted has his birthday on 13th July.

1st	first	January
2nd	second	February
3rd	third	March
4th	fourth	April
5th	fifth	May
6th	sixth	June
7th	seventh	July
8th	eighth	August
9th	ninth	September
10th	tenth	October
11th	eleventh	November
12th	twelfth	December

H Mixed questions

1 Whose birthday is on 3rd January?
2 Whose is on 1st September?
3 When is Ted's birthday?
4 Is Dawn's birthday on 10th December?
5 Is Joanna's on 8th October?
6 Who has his birthday before Vicky?
7 Whose birthday is last in the year?
8 Whose birthday is in the ninth month?

I A birthday party

Do you know the song they are singing? It begins *Happy birthday to you . . .* Write about the birthday party you would like to have.

45

STEP 23
Little Ones

Whales have calves,
Cats have kittens,
Bears have cubs,
Bats have battens,
Swans have cygnets,
Seals have puppies,
But guppies just have
Little guppies.

A Babies

The mother	The baby
cow	calf
dog	puppy
duck	duckling
frog	tadpole
goat	kid
hen	chick
horse	foal
kangaroo	joey
lion	cub
sheep	lamb

Look at the table and then add the right sentence.

**1 A foal is not a baby cow.
It is a baby horse.**

1 A foal is not a baby cow. ......
2 A lamb is not a baby goat. ......
3 A puppy is not a baby cat. ......
4 A kid is not a baby sheep. ......
5 A cub is not a baby dog. ......
6 A duckling is not a baby goose. ......

B What are they?

Ask someone what these babies are.

1 a chick   3 a tadpole   5 a kid
2 a lamb   4 a foal   6 a joey

**1 YOU What is a chick, Tom?
TOM A chick is a baby hen.**

C Complete the sentence

1 Baby lions are called — .
2 Baby dogs are called — .
3 Baby goats are called — .
4 Baby ducks are called — .
5 Baby swans are called — .

D What are they called?

Now write six sentences to say what these are called.

1 baby sheep   4 baby kangaroos
2 baby cats   5 baby whales
3 baby hens   6 baby seals

46

E Little things

ringlet	nestling	kitchenette
streamlet	seedling	mini-skirt

These are the names of six small things.
You will need them to answer these
questions.

Ask someone what each of these is called.

1 a small plant   4 a short skirt
2 a tiny kitchen   5 a baby bird
3 a small stream   6 a small ring
**1   What *is* a small plant called, Ali?
      It is called a seedling.**

F Small quantities

puff   pat   drop   scrap   crumb

These words all name small quantities of
something. *Use them to complete Scatty's
sentences.*

1 I spilt a — of water.
2 I felt a — of wind on my neck.
3 I have a — of paper.
4 I ate a — of bread.
5 I dropped a — of butter.

G Parts of things

Each thing named in the first list is part
of a thing named in the other. *Say what it
is a part of.*

1 A twig is part of a branch.

1 twig	3 page	5 flower
2 door	4 leg	6 wing

book	table	branch
plant	aeroplane	house

H In order

Put each list in order. Say what your order is.

1 house, kitchen, kitchenette, cooker
  (biggest to smallest)
1 kitchenette, cooker, house, kitchen
2 twig, tree, leaf, branch
3 town, village, county, city
4 long dress, mini-skirt, skirt

I Something to write about

*Write about the picture. Write what you can
see, what is happening, and what is going to
happen next. These words will help you.*

farm yard	tractor	pond	pretending
farmer	barn	hay	ducklings
standing	driving	piglets	calf
post	shed	roof	fall down

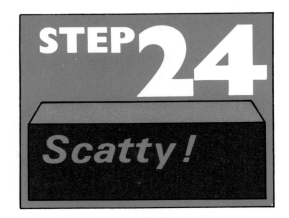

A Picture story

Put these sentences in the right order to tell the story of the pictures.

He sat on one of the branches.
Soon the branch fell to the ground and Scatty, too.
One day Scatty fetched a saw.
He began to saw the branch.
The branch lay on the ground and so did Scatty.
Then he climbed up a tree.

B Questions

1 Where is Scatty in the first picture?
2 What is he carrying?
3 What is he doing in the second picture?
4 Has he started sawing in the third one?
5 What is he doing in the fourth?
6 What is happening in the fifth?
7 Where is Scatty in the last picture?
8 What was Scatty's bad mistake?

C In words

Look at the list of numbers on the opposite page. Then write these in words.

1 twenty three   2 seventeenth

a 23	d 18	g 26th	j 14th
b 17th	e 22nd	h 15	k 29th
c 21st	f 31	i 23rd	l 25

D Odd and even

Say aloud these even and odd numbers, putting in the missing ones.

even   10, 12, 14, ... 20.
odd   1, 3, 5, ... 19.

E Speaking dates

26th February

We write 26th February, but we say
the twenty-sixth of February.
Now you say these dates aloud.

1 17th March	5 28th November
2 23rd January	6 22nd February
3 19th October	7 31st May
4 21st April	8 15th September

F School dates

Term	Starts or finishes	Date
Christmas	starts	7th September
,,	finishes	16th December
Easter	starts	10th January
,,	finishes	31st March
Summer	starts	21st April
,,	finishes	23rd July

This table tells you when Ted's terms
begin and end. *Answer the questions about it.*

1 He starts on 21st April.

1 When does Ted start school in the
  Summer?
2 When does he finish school in the
  Easter term?
3 When does he finish school in the
  Christmas term?
4 When does Ted's Summer term end?
5 When does his Easter term begin?

12	twelve	12th	twelfth
13	thirteen	13th	thirteenth
14	fourteen	14th	fourteenth
15	fifteen	15th	fifteenth
16	sixteen	16th	sixteenth
17	seventeen	17th	seventeenth
18	eighteen	18th	eighteenth
19	nineteen	19th	nineteenth
20	twenty	20th	twentieth
21	twenty-one	21st	twenty-first
22	twenty-two	22nd	twenty-second
23	twenty-three	23rd	twenty-third
24	twenty-four	24th	twenty-fourth
25	twenty-five	25th	twenty-fifth
26	twenty-six	26th	twenty-sixth
27	twenty-seven	27th	twenty-seventh
28	twenty-eight	28th	twenty-eighth
29	twenty-nine	29th	twenty-ninth
30	thirty	30th	thirtieth
31	thirty-one	31st	thirty-first

G The sinking of the Titanic

The *Titanic* was the largest ship in the
world. She was called the 'unsinkable'
Titanic. It was her first trip across the
Atlantic. On 14 April 1912, it happened.
She struck an iceberg at 11 o'clock that
night. Two and a half hours later she sank.
About half of her 2,000 passengers
drowned in the icy water.
Pretend you were on board
and were saved by a life-boat.
Write about what happened.

STEP 25

Doing Words

Can you sing this song?

What's Maria doing now?
Is she playing in the park?
Is she swimming in the pool?
Is she working in her room?
What's Maria doing now?
Is she reading in the lounge?
  She's not playing,
  She's not swimming,
  She's not working,
  She's not reading,
Maria's fast asleep!

TED
TENTSTABLE

KATE

A Warm up

1 Who is swimming?   **1 Leila is.**
2 Who is reading?
3 Who is sleeping?
4 Who is playing football?
5 Who is working in a stable?

ALI
PARK

LEILA
POOL

B Where?

1 Where is Ted reading?   **1 He is reading**
2 Where is Kate working?   **outside his tent.**
3 Where is Ali playing football?
4 Where is Leila swimming?
5 Where is John sleeping?

C Ted and co.

*Write a sentence about each child. Say what
he or she is doing and where.*

1 Ted is reading outside his tent.

JOHN
TREE

D They often do so

The children often do the things they are doing in the photos. Say so.

1 Ted often reads outside his tent.

E They did so yesterday

As a matter of fact, the children did these things yesterday. Say so.

1 Ted read outside his tent yesterday.

F Verbs

Kate worked at the stables yesterday.

Look at the word *worked*. It is a doing word or verb. It tells us what Kate did.

Ali often plays football.

The word *plays* is also a doing word or verb. It tells us what Ali often does. Here are some more verbs:

1 picked	3 sang	5 found
2 kicked	4 drew	6 washed

Pretend you did all these things yesterday. Make a sentence with each verb.

1 I picked some flowers yesterday.

G Using verbs

Choose the best verb to finish each sentence.

1 Monkeys can't write.

1 Monkeys can't — . *(eat, write, drink)*
2 Birds can — . *(draw, talk, fly)*
3 Pigs — . *(grunt, sing, write)*
4 Fish never — . *(eat, drown, swim)*
5 I often — water. *(eat, chew, drink)*
6 Kate often — . *(laughs, drowns, dies)*.

H Alphabetical order

Look at the Little Dictionary on page 64 and try to find a verb for each letter of the alphabet. *Make one long list.*

act, boast, carry, dig ......

I Something to write

Write six sentences about what the children are doing in this picture.

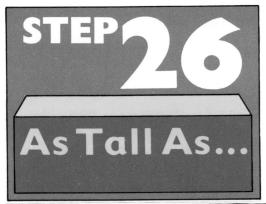

STEP 26

As Tall As...

Tom   Dick   Tracy   George   Linda

A Find the ending

Choose the right ending and make complete sentences.

1 Dick is taller than   Tom and Dick.
2 Tracy is as tall as   George.
3 George is not as tall as   the wall.
4 Tracy is taller than   Tracy.
5 Linda is as tall as   Tom.
6 George is as tall as   Linda.

B Warm up

Answer these questions about the picture.

1 Who is the tallest?
2 Who is the shortest?
3 Which girl is taller than Tracy?
4 Who is as tall as the wall?
5 How many children are taller than Dick?
6 Is Tracy as tall as George?
7 Which girl is shorter than George?
8 Is George taller than Tracy?

C Say it another way

Dick is taller than Tom.
=Tom is not as tall as Dick.

These two sentences have the same meaning. Now write these in the second way.

1 Tracy is taller than Dick.
2 George is taller than Tom.
3 Linda is taller than George.
4 George is taller than Dick.
5 Tom is shorter than Dick.

D The same as

Name	Age	Height	Weight
Wendy	7	102 cm	24 kg
Gary	8	102 cm	22 kg
Wayne	7	110 cm	21 kg
Carole	8	106 cm	22 kg
John	9	110 cm	24 kg

Make sentences by finding the right endings.

1 Wendy is the same weight as   Carole.
2 Gary is the same age as   Gary.
3 Wayne is the same age as   John.
4 Wendy is the same weight as   Wayne.
5 John is the same height as   Wendy.

E Not as . . . as

Carole is not as old as John.
Gary is not as tall as Wayne.
Wayne is not as heavy as Gary.

Make three more sentences like these.

F Who bought what?

Name	Sugar bought
Mrs Brown	2 kg
Mrs White	1 kg
Mrs Black	$\frac{1}{2}$ kg
Mrs Gray	2 kg
Mrs Pink	4 kg
Mrs Green	3 kg

1 **Mrs Black and Mrs White did.**

1 Who bought less sugar than
  Mrs Brown?
2 Who bought most sugar?
3 Who bought less than Mrs White?
4 Which of the ladies bought least sugar?
5 Which of them bought as much as
  Mrs Brown.
6 Who bought 2 kg less than Mrs Pink?
7 Who bought 2 kg more than
  Mrs White?
8 Who bought more than Mrs Brown?

G Missing words

Choose the missing word from this list.
more   less   most   least

1 Mrs Brown bought — sugar than
  Mrs Green.
2 Mrs Pink bought — sugar than
  Mrs Brown.
3 Mrs Black bought — sugar.
4 Mrs Green bought 2 kg — than
  Mrs White.
5 Mrs White bought 2 kg — than
  Mrs Green.
6 Mrs Pink bought — sugar.

H Scatty punctuation

Scatty copied these sentences about Tom
Thumb, but he forgot to put in any
capital letters or punctuation marks.
He should have put in 4 capital letters,
3 full stops and 2 commas. *Write it out
properly for him. When you have done it,
check with Step 13.*

   tom thumb was no bigger than a man's
thumb and he never grew any bigger he
was just 6 cm tall his mother often left
him to play on top of the kitchen table
because she could keep an eye on him
there

I Picture story

The pictures show how Kate found out
what she was as tall as, as wide as and
as heavy as.
*Write down what she did and what she
found out.*

STEP 27
Homes

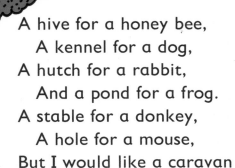

A hive for a honey bee,
  A kennel for a dog,
A hutch for a rabbit,
  And a pond for a frog.
A stable for a donkey,
  A hole for a mouse,
But I would like a caravan
  For my special house.

A Questions

Read the poem to answer these questions.

1 Where do bees live?
2 Is a kennel sometimes a dog's home?
3 Where do frogs live?
4 Do mice live in a hole?
5 Where do donkeys sometimes live?
6 Where would the person who wrote
   the poem like to live?

B People's homes

Where do these people live?
Make six sentences.

1 Kings live in palaces.

1 Kings		tents.
2 Soldiers		convents.
3 Monks	live in	palaces.
4 Nuns		igloos.
5 Campers		barracks.
6 Eskimos		monasteries.

C The homes of creatures

Here are the names of six creatures.

1 a horse	3 a bee	5 a wild rabbit
2 a pig	4 a spider	6 a tiger

And here are the names of their homes.

web	stable	hive
lair	burrow	sty

Write a sentence to say where each creature lives.

1 A horse lives in a stable.

D Something to draw

Some of us live in bungalows, some in country cottages, some in blocks of flats, some in semi-detached houses, some in houses standing on their own. *Which are the buildings in the pictures? Copy them and write under them what they are.*

E Something to find out

Where do these live?

1 whales   3 wasps   5 squirrels

2 foxes   4 eagles   6 Red Indians

F Building a house

Say what is happening in the picture. These words may help:

cement	ladder	roof
concrete	scaffolding	door
bricks	mixer	window
tiles	shovel	timber

G Describe it

Draw a house for yourself to live in. It can be your 'dream' house, if you like. *Write about it.* Perhaps you would like to tell us what it is made of and what it is like inside.

STEP 28
Dictionaries

atlas, a book of maps
breeze, a soft wind
clap, to strike the hands together
damp, not quite dry
deaf, not able to hear
enter, to go in
fetch, to go and get
gander, a male goose
hammer, a tool for hitting nails
holiday, a time when you do not work
huge, very big
island, land with water all round it

A The list of words

The words in the list are in alphabetical order, to help you find them more easily. This is how words are listed in a dictionary. A dictionary tells you what words mean.

With the help of the list, put in the missing word in each of these sentences.

1 A male goose is called a — .
2 A deaf person cannot — .
3 An island is a piece of land with — all round it.
4 A book of maps is called an — .
5 Clothes that are damp are not quite — .
6 A huge crowd is very — .

B Ask someone what each of these is

1 an island   3 a gander   5 an atlas
2 a hammer   4 a breeze   6 a holiday

1 **YOU** What is an island, Bob?
  BOB It is a piece of land with water all round it.

C What does it mean?

Now ask someone what these words mean.

1 fetch   3 huge   5 enter
2 clap   4 deaf   6 damp

1 **YOU** What does fetch mean, Ann?
  ANN It means to go and get.

D A puzzle

Copy this puzzle and then finish it with words from the list.

#								
1	H	U	G	E	■	■		Extremely large
2						■		A book filled with maps
3						■		To go in
4					■	■		Unable to hear
5								You hit nails with it.
6						■		To go and bring back
7								A gentle wind
8					■	■		Slightly wet

E Alphabetical order

These lists are in alphabetical order.

ant	apple
bag	dog
coat	goat
door	zebra

These are not in alphabetical order.

coat	goat
ant	apple
door	dog
bag	zebra

Now put this list in alphabetical order: Karen   Phil   Roger   Reg   Linda.

What did you do about *Roger* and *Reg*?
They both begin with R. So you must go on and look at the next letter in each. Now e comes before o in the alphabet.
So Re comes before Ro and Reg comes before Roger.

F

Put each of these lists in alphabetical order:

1	2	3	4	5	6
Lee	Spain	Leela	Richard	Paris	Lewis
Taylor	France	Jane	Mike	London	Lambert
West	China	Mary	Robert	Moscow	Jones
Roger	India	Louise	Will	Peking	Jacks
Pike	Sweden	Joan	Wayne	Madrid	Jepson

G Use the Little Dictionary
Say who these people are.

1 A chemist is a person who sells medicine.

1 chemist	3 tailor	5 violinist
2 pilot	4 jockey	6 spectator

H Puzzle
See how far you can take this without using the same animal twice.

giraffe   elephant   tiger   reindeer

I An ABC animal story
One day in the forest I met an ant, who met a bear, who met a cat, who met a deer, who . . . *Continue the story.*

fox	mole	elephant	hare
jaguar	goat	kangaroo	opposum
iguana	newt	porcupine	lizard

A Looking at a picture

These words name things in the picture.
See if you can find all twelve of them.

a boy	a bucket	a boat
a girl	a spade	a raft
a dog	a rock	some waves
a seagull	the sun	some clouds

B A long sentence

Cover up the picture and then say what you saw in it just now. Write a long sentence like this:

In the picture I saw a seagull, a dog . . . some waves and a boat.

Remember to put a comma between the words in your list.

, a comma

C What else?

What else did you see in the picture?
Cover up the picture again and then write down the names of five other things in it.

Well, how many did you remember?

D Did you notice?

See how many of these questions you can answer without having to look and see.

1 What colour are your shoes?
2 How many doors are there in the room?
3 Who is the tallest pupil in the class?
4 What colour are the teacher's shoes?
5 Who is the shortest pupil in the class?
6 What colour are your eyes?
7 Did it rain yesterday?
8 What clothes is the teacher wearing?
9 Where is the nearest post box?
10 Who is sitting nearest you?

E Your questions

Think of five new questions to test what your friend has noticed—or not noticed.

F On the scent

How well can you smell?
Put each of these in a paper bag.

chocolate apple coffee onion orange

1 Find out by smell what each bag has in it. Make notes about this.
2 Write about your favourite smells: bacon frying, Dad's pipe smoke, cakes baking, new-mown grass, toast, or what *you* like.

G Listen!

Can you imitate these sounds?
Write about them.

1 Mum calling you indoors.
    being cross with you.
    saying 'Good'.
2 The purr or miaow of a cat.
3 The bark or whine of a dog.
4 Whistles of surprise.
    of joy.
    to call a friend.

If you have a tape recorder, play these sounds into it and make them into a radio play.

a bell ringing
a telephone ringing
a cap-gun shot
water being poured into a glass

H Hard and rough

Bring to school things that are rough, hard, soft or smooth. Sort them out and write a sentence to say which is which.

1 **The penny is hard and smooth.**

Try these or any others.

a penny	a marble	a brick
a feather	a handkerchief	a nail
a sock	a sweet	a file
a stone	a leaf	moss

I Kim's game

Ask the teacher if your group can play Kim's game. Find ten small things to put on a tray. Each of you looks at them for about a minute. Then they are covered up. You write down the names of as many of the things on the tray as you can. The one with the most correct names is the winner.

J Something to write about

Look again at the picture on the opposite page. What did the boy find? How did it get there? What did he do with it? Give the boy a name and write about his finding the treasure.

STEP 30

Give it a Name

a small animal   a medium animal   a big animal

A Big, medium, small

Here are the names of 12 animals.
Sort the animals into three sets of big, medium and small animals.

giraffe	monkey	hamster	squirrel
rabbit	mouse	sheep	mole
cow	elephant	pig	gorilla

B Nouns

Kevin   pencil   wasp   Manchester
These four words are the names of
something, too.

Kevin is the name of a special boy;
pencil is the name of something to write
with;
wasp is the name of a sort of insect;
Manchester is the name of a city.
Kevin, pencil, wasp, Manchester are all nouns.

Words that name something are called
nouns.
Say what each of these nouns is the name of.

1 pie	4 basket	7 England
2 book	5 paper	8 pudding
3 Linda	6 water	9 Tuesday

1 *Pie is the name of something to eat.*

C Name the part

Make two sets of these words.

(1) Parts of a tree   (2) Parts of a house

branch	root	bricks	floor	bud
roof	twig	tiles	kitchen	chimney
wall	ceiling	trunk	flower	window
leaf	door	bark	seed	fruit

D Singular or plural

The noun *brick* means only one brick, and the noun *branch* means only one branch. The noun *bricks* means more than one brick—two, three, or many bricks.

one brick

seven bricks

To make a noun mean more than one—to make it plural—we often add -s:

brick—bricks　　dog—dogs
boy—boys　　word—words

But if the word ends in a hissing sound, we add -es:

branch—branches　　fox—foxes
bush—bushes　　glass—glasses

Make two sets of these nouns:

(1) singular　　(2) plural

boxes	teacher	fishes	bus
toys	brush	girl	donkeys
pie	watches	rats	glass
bird	matches	dish	cages

E Meanings

Look these nouns up in the Little Dictionary and say what each one means.

1 file　　3 deck　　5 kangaroo
2 atlas　　4 gander　　6 ear

1 A file is a tool for smoothing wood or metal.

F Alphabetical order

Write down a noun for each letter of the alphabet. Choose your nouns from the Little Dictionary.

This is how Ted began:

atlas, breeze, chemist, deck . . .

G A word game

The first player starts by saying:
I packed my case and put in it two handkerchiefs. The next player repeats this and adds something else. And so on. Any player who forgets something in the list, or gets the order wrong, drops out. The sixth player might have to say.
I packed my case and put in it two handkerchiefs, a pair of socks, some sweets, a comic, ten marbles and a pair of jeans.

H Greedy Jane

Tell the story of Greedy Jane in the poem.

"Pudding and pie"
Said Jane. "O my!"
　"Which would you rather?"
　Said her father.
"Both!" cried Jane
Quite bold and plain.

STEP 31
Adjectives

KATE An elephant is a very big animal, and a mouse is a very small animal. So what sort of animal is a mole, Scatty?

SCATTY It is a small animal.

KATE Good, And what sort of a puppet are you, Scatty?

SCATTY I am a huge puppet.

KATE No, no, Scatty, you are not huge. What are you?

SCATTY I am not very big and I am not very small.

KATE All right, you are so-so.

SCATTY (sings)
Hello! Hello!
I'm so-so. I'm so-so.
I'm not hot, I'm not cold,
I'm not young, I'm not old.
I'm so-so. That's me.
Good-bye! Good-bye!

A Which?
Look at the monkey, the elephant, the black pig, the pink pig and the mouse. Which one would you call tiny, fat, thin, huge, funny?

1 I would call the mouse tiny.

B What sort of?
What sort of animals are they, then?

1 The monkey is funny.

C Adjectives
Words that tell us about or describe something are called adjectives.
funny, huge, fat, thin and *tiny*
are all adjectives.
Here are some more adjectives. Which things are they most likely to tell us about?
1 a narrow lane.

Adjectives	Nouns
1 narrow	nails
2 cloudy	food
3 rusty	arm-chair
4 tasty	sky
5 fierce	lane
6 comfortable	tigers

D Opposites

An interesting story is the opposite of a boring story. A huge cake is the opposite of a tiny cake.

Find the opposite of each adjective in the first list. Make a sentence to say what it is.

1 Heavy is the opposite of light.
2 Old is the . . . .

1 heavy	small
2 old	hot
3 big	light
4 short	young
5 cold	clean
6 dirty	tall

E What are these the opposites of?

1 A wide road is the opposite of a narrow road.

1 a wide road	4 clean hands
2 a huge room	5 hot milk
3 a heavy case	6 a cruel man

F

Give each of these adjectives its right meaning. Check with the Little Dictionary.

1 cruel,   very unkind

1 cruel	very big
2 damp	very strong
3 deaf	not quite dry
4 feeble	very unkind
5 huge	not able to hear
6 powerful	weak

G Written sentences

Say what sort of things these are. Use the Little Dictionary to help. For the second one you must look up the word wooden.

1 A ripe apple is one that is ready to eat.

1 a ripe apple	4 lean meat
2 a wooden spoon	5 a comical story
3 a powerful car	6 a shallow stream

H Lots of adjectives

Dogs can be obedient, noisy, greedy, fierce, muddy, friendly, naughty, black, white, brown, big, small, hungry, tired . . .
Now say what you think these can be:

1 boys   2 cats   3 sweets

I Put them in alphabetical order

1 bare, busy, early, empty, light.

1 empty, bare, early, busy, light.
2 soft, hard, shallow, large, new.
3 round, risky, strict, smooth, poor.
4 great, funny, good, high, friendly.
5 thin, tall, timid, terrible, true

J Something to write about

*Say what your favourite pet is like.
Or say what the thing you hate most is like.
Use all the adjectives you can.*

A Little Dictionary

act, to take a part on the stage

atlas, a book of maps

boast, to praise oneself

breeze, a soft wind

carry, to take in one's arms

chemist, a person who sells medicine

clap, to strike the hands together

comical, funny; making you laugh

cruel, very unkind

damp, not quite dry

deaf, not able to hear

deck, the part of a ship you stand on

dig, to turn over the soil

ear, the part of the body you hear with

enter, to go in

feeble, weak

fetch, to go and get

file, a tool for smoothing wood or metal

gander, a male goose

greedy, wanting to eat too much

grunt, to make a noise like a pig

hammer, a tool for hitting nails

holiday, a time when you do not work

huge, very big

hum, to sing with the mouth closed

inform, to tell

island, land with water all round it

jockey, a person who rides race horses

juggle, to do clever tricks

kangaroo, an Australian animal that jumps on its hind legs

kick, to strike with the foot

lasso, a rope for catching cattle or horses

lean, without any fat

lick, to touch or wipe with the tongue

mock, to make fun of

mutton, meat from a sheep

nibble, to eat in little pieces

nose, part of the body you smell with

oar, a wooden bar to row with

observe, to look at carefully

pilot, a person who flies an aeroplane

powerful, very strong

practise, to do something over and over again.

queue, a line of people waiting for something

racket, a bat for playing tennis

remember, to keep in mind

ripe, ready to eat

scamper, to run about quickly

shallow, not very deep

spectator, a person who looks on

surly, rude and bad-tempered

tailor, a person who makes clothes

tickle, to touch a person to make him laugh

umpire, a judge in a game

upset, to turn something over

violinist, a person who plays the violin

vomit, to be sick

wheat, the seed from which bread is made

wipe, to dry or clean with a cloth

wooden, made of wood

x-ray, to photograph the inside of the body

xylophone, bars that are struck to make music

yacht, a sailing boat

yell, to shout loudly

zebra, a striped animal like a small horse

zig-zag, to move from side to side